MY FIRST

VALENTINE'S DAY BOOK

by Marian Bennett
illustrated by Pam Peltier

created by The Child's World

CHILDRENS PRESS ™

CHICAGO

Library of Congress Cataloging in Publication Data

Bennett, Marian.
   My first Valentine's Day book.

   Summary: Poems describe Valentine's Day experiences,
such as the school party, greeting the mailman, and
family dessert.
   1. Valentine's Day—Juvenile poetry.   2. Children's
poetry, American.   [1. Valentine's Day—Poetry.
2. American poetry]   I. Peltier, Pam, ill.   II. Child's
World (Firm)   III. Title.
PS3552.E54738M9   1985   811'.54   84-21511
ISBN 0-516-02906-1

MY FIRST

VALENTINE'S DAY BOOK

Valentine's Day

"Mommy," I asked,
"Why do we have Valentine's Day?"

Mommy said, "It's a day to let
people know you love them.
Sometimes you tell them.
Sometimes you give them a gift.
Best of all, you do something special
    for them."

I thought about my friends.
How could I say, "I love you?"

Valentine,
how can I make
you see that
you're simply
tops with
me?

Buying Valentines

My piggy bank
   isn't fat any more.
I took my money
   to the valentine store.
I gave the lady
   my nickels and dimes,
   and she gave me
      pretty valentines—
      valentines for my friends.

—Colleen L. Reece

Be
my
valentine!

Making Valentines

Bright red paper,
lots of paste,
shiny scissors,
frilly lace.
Fold and cut,
take your time,
that's how to make
   a valentine.

                —Colleen L. Reece

There's a place
in my heart
just for you.

A Valentine Box

I'm making the most beautiful
box in the world—
wait and see.
My sister is helping me.
When we're done,
I'll take it to school
where my friends
will stuff it full.
At least. . .
I hope there will be
lots of valentines for me.

—*Colleen L. Reece*

11

Dressing Up

It's time to go to school.
We're going to have a
    Valentine party.
I can hardly wait!
Mommy said I could wear
    my new red dress and
    shiny black shoes.
I feel pretty.
My Valentine cards are all
    ready.
So is my box.

A Valentine Party

Our party is fun!
We have cookies that look
  like hearts.
We have red punch too.
I have to be careful to
  keep my dress clean.
Whoops! Jimmy just spilled
  his punch.
Amber dropped one of her
  cookies.
I haven't spilled anything.
This is a good party!

My Box

Look! My box is full of cards.
I'm going to open it and look
   at the cards.
Here's a card from Amy.
She's my best friend.
This card says, "Be mine."
   I can read that.
I can read the name too—
            Brian.
I think Brian likes me!

A Valentine for Teacher

My teacher's name is Miss Sharon.
I like her a lot. She's pretty.
I bought her a special card.
It says, "To my teacher."
I printed my name on it.

Miss Sharon looked at the card.
Then she smiled at me and said,
   "Thank you, Ben."
Now she knows how much I like her.
I think she likes me too.

"To my Teacher."

The Mailman

When I get home from school,
  it is time for the mail carrier.
His name is Mr. Smith.
He's my friend.
  "Hi, Mr. Smith.
  Do you have some mail
  for me?" I ask.
He smiles as he gives me a
  handful of letters.
"And here's a package for you,"
  he says. "Somebody must
  love you!"

Do you love me or do
you not?
You told me once,
but I forgot!

Valentine Gift

Rip! goes the paper.
Pop! goes the ribbon.
Oh, it's a teddy bear!
He has a heart around
   his neck.
The heart says,
   "Happy Valentine's Day.
   We love you.
      Grandpa and Grandma."
I give Teddy a hug.
I wish I could give Grandpa
   and Grandma a hug!

23

Valentine Candy

On Valentine's Day
Daddy gives each of
    us a heart-shaped,
    box of candy.
Billy reads aloud
    from some of his
    little hearts:
"Be mine." "I love you."
"All my love." "Sweetheart."
I'd rather eat mine than
    read them.

Kitty's Valentine

Valentines are so much fun!
I even made my kitten one!
I made it red and trimmed it
   with lace,
      and put it in her special
      place.
With it I put some balls of thread
   in valentine colors of white and red.
My card said,
   "To my favorite pet!
   Happy Valentine's Day!"

Valentine Surprises

Guess what we are having for
    my party — a big heart-cake
    with sugar roses.
Mommy baked it just for me!
After the party, I
    will surprise Mommy.
I will do the dishes —
    all by myself!
Won't that be a good surprise?
    I like Valentine's Day!

A Special Valentine

After dinner, I took
    a special valentine next door
    to my special friend, Mrs. Johnson.
She lives alone and always does
    special things for me!

Giving a valentine
is so much fun —
It's almost as good
as getting one!

31